Betty
Peggy
Barbara
Joan
Janet
Jarrett
Kay
Margaret
Dee

An Artist's Safari

Impala ram

This book was first published in 1970. I was fortunate to make this safari in East Africa before the Federation broke up and the different countries went their separate ways. It is, of course, still possible to see the parks mentioned in the book.

This new edition is published in a format which, it is hoped, will be much more convenient to handle. It should therefore be easier to examine the pen drawings, and it is these which I regard as the kernel of the book. Although some of the colour plates are now shown as single-page 'details' only, it is to be hoped that this more manageable format will make the new Artist's Safari a welcome successor to the first edition.

R.T.

Ralph Thompson

An Artist's Safari

Impala

COLLINS · ST JAMES'S PLACE · LONDON
in association with The Tryon Gallery
1979

This book is dedicated to all those
who work for the conservation of
wild life.

By the same author: A BRUSH WITH ANIMALS (Rupert Hart-Davies)

ISBN 0 00 211033 4
© Ralph Thompson 1970 and 1979
First published in 1970 in landscape format
by William Collins Sons and Co Ltd
London · Glasgow · Sydney · Auckland
Toronto · Johannesburg in association
with The Tryon Gallery

This edition first published 1979

Filmset by Keyspools Ltd, Golborne, Lancs
Reproduction by New Era Studios, London
Printed in Great Britain by Ebenezer Baylis & Son Ltd,
Leicester and London
Bound by Hunter & Foulis Ltd, Edinburgh

Acknowledgements

NAIROBI

My wife and I wish to thank all our many friends in East Africa who made us so very welcome and whose advice helped us to plan our safari.

When, owing to unforeseen circumstances, we were left at the very last moment without bookings and without a car, Mr. Oliver Brooke swiftly made arrangements for us through Brooke Bond Travel Limited. Oliver and his wife Betty most wisely insisted that I should not attempt to drive as well as sketch, and gave us the services of Martin Ondu, one of their best couriers. Martin seemed to have two pairs of eyes, one for the road and another for animals and birds. We are deeply indebted to him too for dealing with all the chores and worries of our journey and for taking such wonderful care of us throughout. The Brookes also flew us to Samburu in the company's plane and whilst there, drove us everywhere in their own land-rovers.

NGURDOTO CRATER, LAKE MANYARA AND THE SERENGETI

In Arusha, Mr. John Owen, Director of the Tanzanian National Parks, very generously put the staff guest houses at Lake Manyara and the Serengeti at our disposal, and gave us free access for study in the parks with skilled guides to help us.

MASAI MARA

At the Masai Mara Game Park, we were indebted to the late Major Lyn Temple-Boreham, Senior Game Warden, Narok District, and his wife Joan. For several days he gave generously of his time, and his long experience and wide background knowledge of African wildlife.

Without the friendship and invaluable help of all these people, many of the sketches in this book would never have been made.

I must also thank our African guides, but for whose skill, many interesting subjects and experiences would have been missed.

I would like to thank Mr. Dudley Blunt of John Dickinson and Company Limited for providing such a formidable pile of sketch books which by the end of the safari proved none too many. Miss Winwood Reade gave me invaluable help here in England with the written account of the safari, for which I am most grateful.

And above all, I wish to thank my wife, 'Bill', for sharing experiences of every kind in Africa, the beauty of the early mornings, the magic of the hour before sunset, identifying a new bird, or even waiting patiently in the heat of the car for some animal to change its position. And then, when the excitements were all over, for patiently helping to sort and choose the sketches and material for this book.

Route by road
Route by plane

Lake B[...]

EQUATOR

Lake Na[...]

LAKE VICTORIA

Lake [...]

Migration herds of Zebra
Wildebeest and Buffalo
and the predators.

NAROK

THE MASAI MARA

Keekerok Lodge

Seronera Lodge

Lake
Natron

THE SERENGETI

Leopard, Lion,
and Cheetah
Plain's game.

Ngorongoro
Crater

(Lions in trees
Elephant
Tropical forest
Lakeside scene)

Lake N[...]

LAKE MANYARA

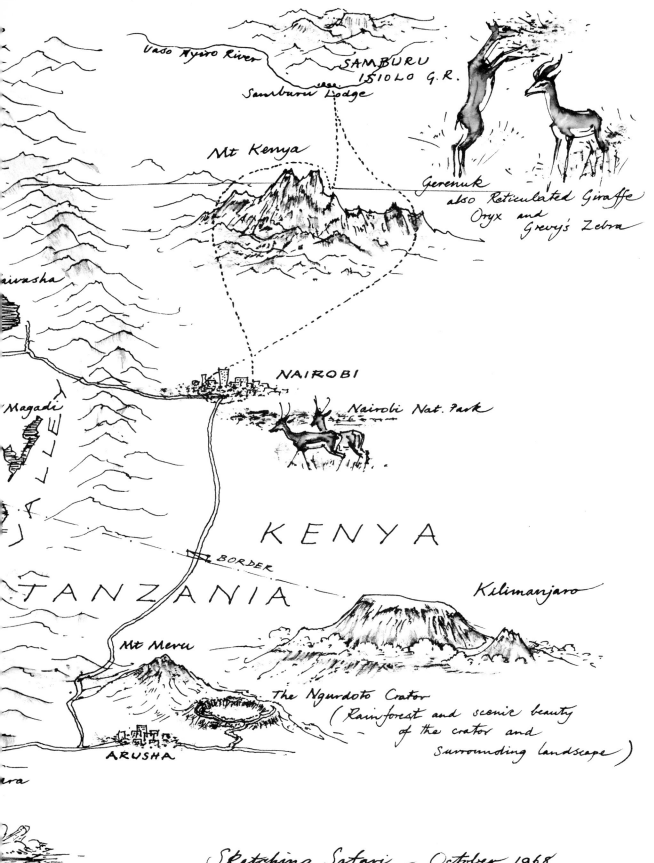

Vaso Nyiro River

SAMBURU
ISIOLO G.R.

Samburu Lodge

Mt Kenya

Gerenuk
also Reticulated Giraffe
Oryx and
Grevy's Zebra

NAIROBI

Nairobi Nat. Park

aivasha

Magadi

VALLEY

KENYA

BORDER

Kilimanjaro

TANZANIA

Mt Meru

The Ngurdoto Crater
(Rainforest and scenic beauty
of the crater and
surrounding landscape)

ARUSHA

ara

Sketching Safari — October 1968.

Introduction

I had one compelling reason to go to Africa. I had reached a moment in my work when I had to walk out of my studio, leaving behind studies made in zoos and museums, in order to steep myself in all the varied sights, sounds and scents of animals living in the full freedom of their natural environment. This book is an informal record of my recent safari in East Africa.

Time is essential if one is to tune in to the visual wavelength of a place. Experience has shown me that I must have time to stand and stare, to watch day after day, making sketches and written notes of anything and everything that compels my attention, whether it be a wild flower or a herd of elephant. So I resisted the temptation to rush around and take a quick look at as much of Africa as possible, and instead I selected only three or four areas in which to concentrate my work.

I had heard much of Lake Manyara National Park, a small reserve wedged between the lake itself and the rift-valley escarpment. Here I would see the different landscape backgrounds of the lakeside, the high cliffs of the escarpment and the tropical forest with its giant trees. But I had another reason for wanting to visit Lake Manyara. It is one of the very few places in Africa where lions have learned to climb trees; the sight of a tawny lioness lolling in the branches of an accacia tree would, I felt sure, be a striking subject to paint. And on the way I would have a chance to see the forest country of the small but very beautiful Ngurdoto Crater National Park near Arusha.

Of all the cat family, the leopard is probably my favourite, but it is also the most elusive to track down. The Serengeti, I knew, would give me the best chance to study them, as well as cheetah and lion. I also wanted to see the great herds of zebra and wildebeest which in October—when I would be there—would have already migrated north and west. If I could include the Masai Mara Reserve, which lies north of the Serengeti across the Tanzania–Kenya border, I would then see something of them.

These parts are on well-established tourist routes. I decided that, to round off the safari, I wanted something a little off the beaten track and so I chose Samburu. Here, north of Mount Kenya and close to the country where Joy Adamson's Elsa lived, I would find a whole new range of flora and fauna.

The wildlife in many areas of Africa continues today much as it has done for thousands of years, thanks very largely to the foresight, constant hard work and sacrifice of a growing number of people. As the days went by, I was caught up in the timeless world of the bush. And yet, as I watched this richly varied spectacle, I found that each day was full of the unexpected, of exciting impressions that presented themselves and a moment later were replaced by others. A good zoological collection can give some

idea of the immense range of birds and animals to be seen there, but it can never convey the inter-related rhythms of Africa, the shapes, colours and movements that surround you. There is so much a zoo can never show: the astonishingly smooth articulation of limb of a herd of elephant on the move, the formidable thundering charge of a herd of buffalo, or the breathless soaring leap of impala fleeing through thorn scrub; while the comical waddling gait of pelicans in captivity is replaced by graceful flotillas sailing on the wind-ruffled surface of a lake, or glorious effortless flight above one's head.

But there is something else, too, in the African bush; there is always a tension, an alertness so hard to describe but which I find deeply moving; 'a craning of the neck', Martin Buber called it, of creatures living their own lives in their own surroundings. It is revealed in the bright eye, the alert stance, the poise of the head on the curve of the neck, or even the flick of an ear.

All this presents the artist with formidable technical problems. A cine-camera provides one way of making a record, but then the eye is imprisoned behind the viewfinder. But in my experience the very effort of making rapid sketches brings me closer to the scene in front of me. There is a feeling of participation, a sense almost of being part of it.

Speed is essential. I use a fountain pen, because the pen-line cannot give a blurred impression, and by declaring itself instantly to be right or wrong, it stimulates a decisive response, forcing hand and eye to a greater clarity. A touch with a moistened finger to the line gives a modifying tone or accent to the drawing where needed. In the evening I look through the day's drawings, sometimes daring to add a touch to strengthen or clarify an impression while it is still fresh in my mind.

The sketch is the first intuitive impression of something seen, the earliest statement of an idea, a pose, gesture or scene, that may one day develop into a painting. Sometimes it will lie in the studio for years waiting for some new impression to join with it, clarifying the ideas it contains and making them clear enough for further development.

The book, then, is a collection of some of the thousands of sketches made on the safari, together with some paintings which have already developed from them showing the relationship of sketch to painting. But the sketches, being my instinctive and immediate response to what I saw, form a language of their own, giving an impression of Africa which, for me, cannot be expressed in any other way. In editing the sketches for this book I have naturally chosen the more complete and intelligible, but I have also included some of the more fragmentary ones, and others which reflect the pressure of coping with too many subjects at once. I have added a simple colour wash to a few of the drawings but, by and large, the sketches that follow are just as they appear on my pad at the end of the day.

Nairobi

First Impressions

It was late September when my wife and I landed at Nairobi and at once we set off for the Westwood Park Country Club, some ten miles away. We had particularly asked for somewhere quiet, and were delighted to find that our bungalow was separated from the main club buildings by an avenue of bougainvillea and shady trees. The smiling houseboy who carried our baggage was a little puzzled because we chose to sleep in the smallest bedroom, but there were nests of weaver birds only a few feet from the window, and we could look out across a wild valley, with glimpses of a stream flanked by plumes of papyrus.

When you are uprooted suddenly from familiar surroundings, it takes time to get your bearings; during the next few days, some part of ourselves, left behind by the speed of the journey, found its own way to Africa and I was ready to start work.

Fresh surroundings stimulate the eye to re-examine the visual world, and when one travels to a new continent, even the familiar looks strange. As we sat in the sunshine or strolled over to the club for meals, we started to learn a new visual language. All around, the birds, trees, butterflies and animals were so different. Against shades of bougainvillea, varying from pale orange to deep crimson, drifted a large swallowtail butterfly. Two or three tiny birds, their dominant colour a brilliant azure blue, alighted in the grass at the foot of a bottle-brush tree; we identified them later as the red-cheeked cordon-bleu, members of the waxbill family. Sudden movements at the foot of the birdtable drew our attention to a delightful family of striped mice leaping high over each other in their hurry to seize scraps of food before bounding away into the shrubbery.

Walks near the bungalow led to many discoveries. Once, there was a whirring sound, a blur of wings, and something shot past me and landed in the grass; it had disappeared so completely that all I could do was to search the spot where it had vanished. After a few moments I detected a shape which seemed different

Locust

Augur Buzzard

from the surrounding pattern of grass stems and fallen leaves: it was a locust, almost three inches long. Its fearsome insect beauty matched its terrible history of destruction. Later, when I was examining some curiously shaped seedpods lying under a tree, I came on a black grasshopper, beautifully jewelled with minute points of ruby and emerald which I caught in a tumbler to sketch.

A flock of brownish birds, with long tail-feathers streaming out behind them, flew into an acacia tree and immediately started stripping off the flowers. They had broad finch-like beaks, handsome crests, speckled plumage with pale underparts, and they climbed rather than hopped among the branches. It is this curious manner of clambering among the twigs that at once explains why they are called 'mouse-birds'. I quickly became familiar with the fiscal shrike and the augur buzzard, with weaver birds, bul-buls and the African golden oriole, and each succeeding day brought more birds that were new to me.

To the zoologist, plants are important because they form the basis of food-chains on which all animal life depends, but to the artist, they have another significance; they have a beauty all their own, but they are also necessary to complete a painting as they provide a detail in the foreground perhaps, or give an indication of the habitat where the animal is normally seen.

The valley gave me opportunities to make studies of various grasses and wild flowers. One of the most striking plants I saw had an orange, daisy-like flower, through the centre of which thrust another length of stem with a bud at the tip; often there were as many as four or five flowers on one stem, like a series of coloured beads on a string. The corolla is said to resemble the ear of a lion—hence the name *Leonotis*—but at a later stage, when the petals have fallen, it is even more decorative with round, bristly, tawny seed heads. In the wooded part of the valley there were many flowering trees and shrubs; a lovely and familiar scent led us to a wild jasmine. In the evening, as we lingered outside the bungalow in the fading light, the soft air seemed to be laden with scent. The perfume from a shrub called 'Yesterday, Today and Tomorrow', with dark blue flowers that bleached white in a few days, was particularly pervasive at this hour.

Striped mice under bird table

With darkness, the sounds of the night took over; a chorus of bell-like clarity began as the frogs tuned up and varied their rhythm. Each night we were woken by hideous noises, grating and disturbing, one deep-toned call answered by a chorus of higher pitched notes from across the valley. They were sometimes so close that I went out with a torch, only to hear the sound move away around the treetops towards the valley. We learnt that this frightful din was made by the tree hyrax, an odd little animal which we did not catch a glimpse of until later.

At dawn, the tree outside the window stood out dark and motionless against an orange sky. Suddenly, the nests and the tips of the branches swayed quickly from side to side as one after another the weaver birds darted off to begin their day.

Nairobi National Park

The National Park is only a few miles south of Nairobi, and though relatively small in area, it has a wonderful variety of habitats and therefore a wide range of animal life. With subjects appearing and disappearing so quickly, I had to keep my sketchbook open on my knees with my fountain pen at the ready. The fact that several fascinating animal movements can occur almost simultaneously stimulates concentration. The eye is forced to select the bare essentials, the hand to respond with a few swift lines and in the excitement of the moment of drawing, there is no sense of effort. Sometimes the results are incomprehensible, but at others they give the shorthand notes I need for work in the studio.

I am always on the look-out for natural forms, beautiful in themselves, that seem to typify a particular place. A low growing, bush-like form of acacia is very common on the plains of East Africa and, to me, *Acacia drepanolobium* or 'whistling thorn', is a perfect symbol of this landscape. It takes its name from the sound of the wind vibrating the long thorns and whistling across the holes in the galls. From the aesthetic point of view I found the shape of the black galls, with a pair of 'steely' thorns growing from them, very satisfying; the complete plant would make excellent foreground material for paintings.

Visitors to the game parks are, of course, confined to their cars at all times. To the artist, this can present problems. I manoeuvred the car up to the thorn

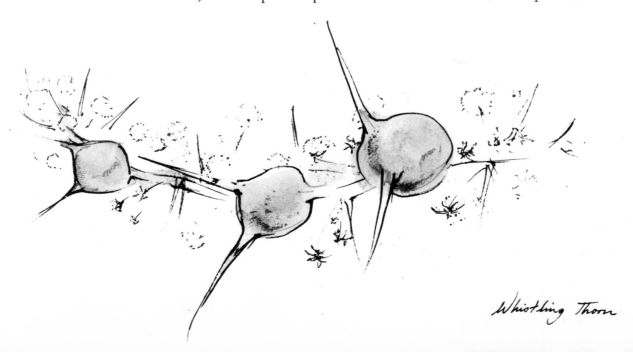

Whistling Thorn

bush and leaned out to break off a spray and get a closer look. Immediately my fingers, hand and arm were swarming with tiny ants, which could both bite and sting. I should have remembered that the galls provide a safe breeding place for insects. I quickly put the spray on the bonnet of the car at a suitable angle for drawing but a fresh wind constantly changed its position and threatened to blow it away. I then trapped the heel of the spray, with the ants safely outside, by winding up the window tightly; this, however, did not give me a good drawing position and so I left the whistling thorn to blow in the breeze and drove on. When I got home that evening, I found that all the ants had gone and at last I was free to make my sketch.

goslings —
Egyptian Goose

Serval

The Animal Orphanage

The orphanage, which is run by the staff of the park, gave me an opportunity to make studies of animals at close quarters, including some that are not often seen. When I was there, a family of servals, mother and kittens, were my chief delight. The serval is smaller than the better known leopard or cheetah. It has something of the lynx about it, with long legs, a short tail and large pointed ears. I am told that even tame servals remain inexorably wild in temperament. With its beautifully marked tawny fur and distinctive expression, it makes a fine subject.

dull grey pink round eyes
r darn nose

grey   white moustache

Blue Monkey

Lesser Kudu

A pair of serval kittens

Ngurdoto Crater National Park

Tanzania

A Wildlife Sanctuary

About twenty miles from Arusha and lying at the foot of Mt. Meru there is a crater said to have been extinct for a quarter of a million years. It is now a wildlife sanctuary and part of the Ngurdoto Crater National Park. Visitors are not allowed into the four square miles of the crater bowl, but from the forest road which climbs around the rim, they can look down on what is virtually a secret world of animals. When visibility is good, there are spectacular views of Mt. Kilimanjaro from look-out points. Our schedule allowed for one long morning here, time enough to look, but only to do brief sketches.

On the forest road leading up to the rim, vervet monkeys watched our approach inquisitively. When they stood up to get a better look at us, they changed suddenly from the little grey monkeys I was familiar with, to tall slender figures, white all the way down from the ruffs around their black faces to their black paws, so that for a moment I didn't recognise them. A mile or so farther on, we stopped by a stream to watch a giant kingfisher perched on a twig only a few yards from the car. With speckled plumage on a smallish body, a remarkably large head and dagger-like bill, I found myself having to check its proportions again and again.

After passing the park gates and climbing steeply towards tall trees and lush vegetation, we had a sudden glimpse of a small group of colobus monkeys, sitting high up in the branches of an almost leafless tree. In the strong light,

Vervet monkey

their long white capes and the white fringe round their faces looked gay and startling against the rich black of their fur; with enormous white plumes at the end of their tails, the total effect was decidedly comical. This illustrates one of the difficulties facing an artist. The immense variety of markings and patternings on birds and animals can be baffling to the eye because often they break up outlines and disguise the essential shape: at the same time, they add enormously to the interest of wildlife subjects.

Three more monkeys emerged one after the other from the dense foliage of a neighbouring tree-top and launched themselves in the direction of the leafless tree. There followed a series of spectacular drops and leaps. All feeling of comedy vanished as their tail plumes and capes streamed out, creating a striking impression of gliding and parachuting from astonishing heights.

As we drove up the narrow road through the forest, again and again we heard and then caught sight of the white-naped raven. We also watched a crested hawk-eagle and a troop of baboons. Farther still, we glimpsed a large hornbill flapping about in a tree-top. The effect was startling. Accustomed to the more sombre shades of woodland birds in England, we were now surrounded by countless brilliantly coloured forest birds.

As I stood at one of the vantage points looking out over the crater I had a wonderful sense of belonging to another world. High above and beyond the

grey-spotted with white

white

White throat
chestnut breast
White abdomen speckled under wings.

Giant Kingfisher

Colobos Monkeys

— on forest road climbing up
towards rim of Ngurdoto Crater

crater, Mt. Meru disappeared and re-appeared through shrouds of slowly drifting
clouds; below, the soft greens and golds of the sanctuary were framed by the
graceful trees around the rim. The setting was almost park-like, unlike anything
I had seen in Africa so far and, in terms of landscape painting, it reminded me
of the work of Claude Lorrain, and Turner would have revelled in it. Two or
three miles away along the farthest stretch of the crater's floor, numerous black
specks became a large herd of buffalo when we saw them through our binoculars. Below us, a solitary rhino looked like a minutely fashioned toy; some
brown dots some distance to the right of the rhino became warthogs rootling
in soft marshy ground among reed stems.

Around my feet was the detailed world of leaves and grasses, with tiny tree
frogs, barely an inch long, beautifully camouflaged amongst the dead leaves.
Blue dragon-flies made urgent zig-zag flights across the green turf. There were
grasshoppers and a dark blue wasp buzzing here and there, but it was the

gorgeous butterflies which seemed to belong most to the particular beauty of the place.

We found elephant dung, some old, and some recent, but no elephants. Presently, Martin Ondu, our courier, turned the car and drove us off round the crater to find the highest point. We stopped to watch a colony of brilliant chestnut-breasted bee-eaters darting in and out of a dozen round nest holes in a sandy bank by the road. From the fork of a tall tree heavily festooned with moss, a solitary monkey sat watching us. It was dark blue-black except for a grey fringe round its face. We identified it later as a blue monkey, closely related to the Sykes monkey. In another tree-top, shaggy with moss and tree ferns, we could see a lot of movement, accompanied by noisy disturbances. I could not pick out any definite shapes but Martin assured me that they were fruit bats.

Farther on up the slope, a slight movement in the bushes brought the car to a halt. About five paces away, through a gap in the foliage, appeared the massively horned head of a buffalo, and behind were the other members of the herd. Evidently the buffalo were moving along their own hidden trails around the crater rim. The visual impact was one of primitive power and massive

Mt Meru and Ngurdoto Crater

weight. One sensed the agelessness of a primitive beast, and recognised the latent power and vitality recorded in early cave drawings. I knew that there could be only a few moments in which to steady myself in order to observe the craggy mass of forehead, the gleam of light on the moist nostril, the rising symmetry of horns and then to note the patterning of beasts against each other and against the background of trees. For one long moment, man and beast eyed each other warily. The only movement was the flap of a shaggy ear. Then the moment of surprise became a moment of danger, which we all felt instinctively. Martin let in the clutch. As we drove off discreetly, I looked back and caught glimpses of the herd heaving and shouldering each other as they turned and trundled off behind the screen of trees.

The road continued to climb and eventually when the car could take us no farther, we scrambled up the last hundred feet to the highest point. Looking out over the golden brown distance, patterned with cloud shadows, a great flat topped mass of distant cloud told us where Kilimanjaro lay hidden. It was too late in the day for a clear view but, as if to compensate us, a pair of swallowtail butterflies danced in the sunshine, bright blue against the whiteness of the cloud.

Lake Manyara National Park

Bungalow beneath a Baobab Tree

After the dense rain forest of the crater and the fertile plantations of coffee and banana around the town of Arusha, the drive westwards over the plains to Lake Manyara presented a picture of desolation. At this time of year, when the short rains are expected, the Masai herdsmen burn away great stretches of dead grass believing that it helps new growth. Sometimes the flames, racing before the wind, were right beside us as we drove along and the horizon was always blue with smoke haze. Sometimes the fire had moved ahead of us and birds were already searching the charred ground and patches of scorched scrub for dead insects.

It was a relief to see the gleam of Lake Manyara in the distance, with the wall of the Rift Valley escarpment behind it. As we drew nearer we saw the first real sign of habitation since we had left Arusha early that afternoon: banana plantations, and among them the busy village of Mto Wa Mbu (Mosquito Creek). A throng of brightly dressed Africans crowded around the open stalls. We bought a week's supply of tinned food from a store crammed with wares of every kind, while from a row of stalls, gay with fruit and vegetables, Martin bargained for huge tomatoes, oranges, bananas and paw paws.

It was only a short drive from the village to the staff guest house which John Owen, Director of the Tanzania National Parks, had kindly arranged for our use. The house is one of the group of buildings from which the Manyara National Park is administered, and it stands apart on high ground. The veranda was deeply shaded by thickets of bamboo and trees, with a long clear view over the banana plantations to a brown and gold landscape, with the road we had travelled threading its way back through blackened patches of earth towards the hills into the smoky distance.

the Dessert Rose   a Impala Lily

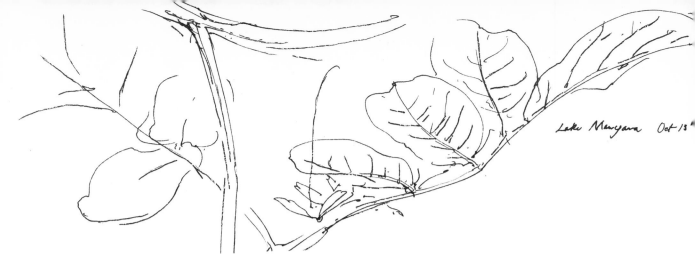

A baobab tree dominated the low building. Some say that God planted the baobab tree upside down because it looks as if the roots were in the air instead of the branches. Certainly everything about its appearance is mysterious. The bark is a cold, silky grey, warmed by a strange violet colour. Two large clusters of creamy-yellow and orange orchids grew from the giant limbs of our tree, and weaver birds had built their nests at the tips of the long drooping branches. Growing between the baobab tree and a tall cactus, we found the crimson-edged flowers of the desert rose. This rare succulent is sometimes known as the impala lily.

From the branch of a broad-leaved tree close to the bungalow door, hung a delicate cocoon woven out of dried grasses and decorated with a few faded red petals. In the small round entrance hole at the top of this we often saw the owner of the nest sitting inside, a handsome little sunbird, whose head only was visible with one bright eye watching us.

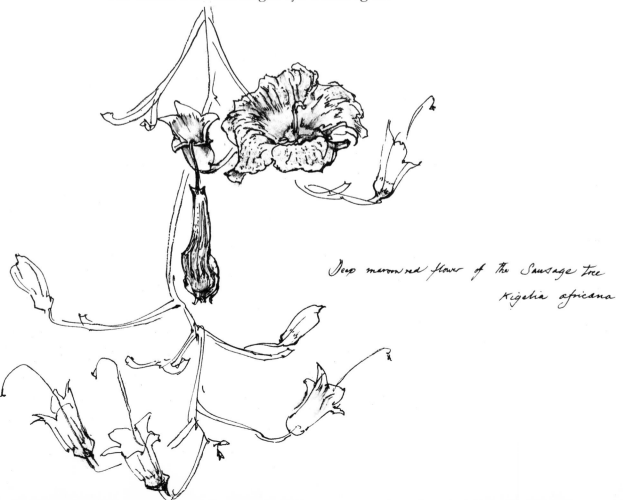

Deep maroon red flower of the Sausage Tree
Kigelia africana

Sunbird in nest

The guest house was ideal for my purpose. It was roomy and quiet and full of character and atmosphere. If the bathwater was a curious reddish brown, it was at least hot and refreshing after a day's work. From the bedroom window at the back I could look up at the variety of trees covering the lower slopes of the escarpment. Thickets of bamboo screened us from all signs of activity at the park head-quarters. We were comfortingly close yet living in a secret world of our own.

At dusk, sunbirds and weaver birds disappeared, bats took over and frogs began a chorus nearby. I found several pairs of tiny gecko lizards on the walls of our rooms. They were too high up for me to sketch so I had to stand on a chair to draw them. If in my eagerness I came too close, they streaked away and I had to stalk them all over again. At night our sleep was disturbed by hideous screeching noises, rising to shrill crescendos, not from tree hyraxes this time but from fruit bats. It was towards dawn that for the first time on our safari we heard the roar of lions not very far away.

Wild figtree – buttress roots –

The Forest Area

Shallow streams and rivulets flow from the foot of the rift escarpment and spread out into the forest area. Because of this seepage of water from the volcanic rock, the forest trees grow to enormous heights. The trees, however, are not festooned with moss and lichen like those of the rain forest because the atmosphere is not sufficiently humid. Below them a star-shaped reed grows in profusion. Dappled here and there by brilliant patches of sunlight, the dark greens of the forest became darker in the recesses and sometimes I felt there was something a little sinister about these heavily shaded depths.

The size of the trees gave a new scale to familiar animals like the elephant and the giraffe. A gigantic fig tree dwarfed a group of waterbuck. A pair of rhino browsed in the dense undergrowth. Silvery-cheeked hornbills flapped clumsily high above our heads and a number of Sykes monkeys were gathering wild figs.

*rhino browsing on palm
in forest area*

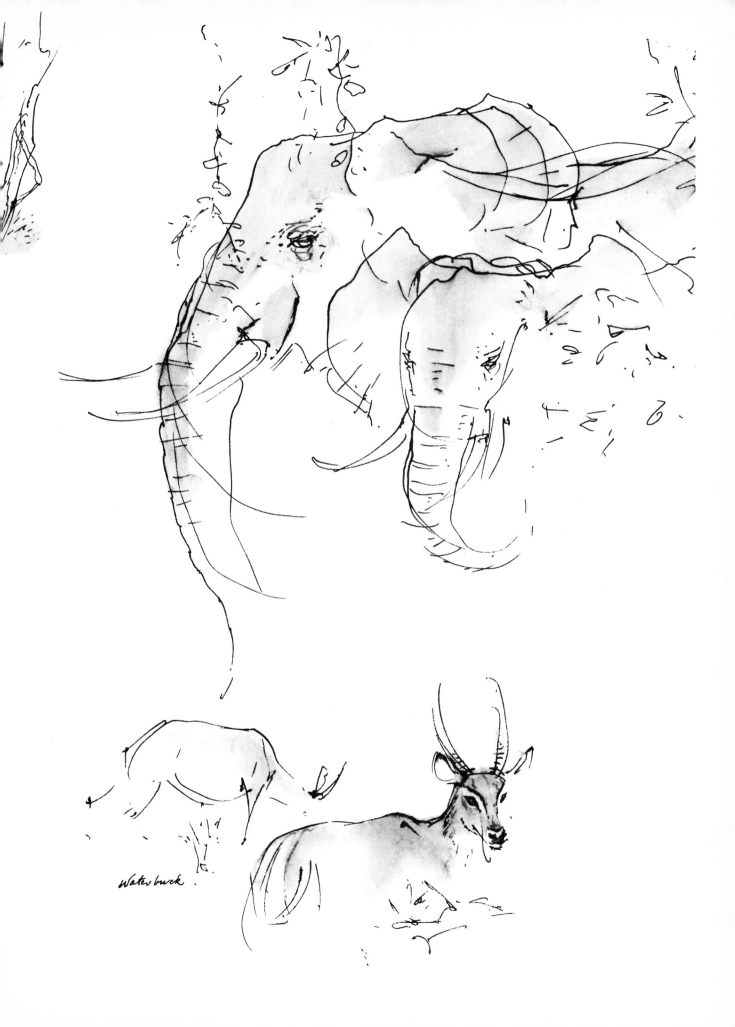

Waterbuck.

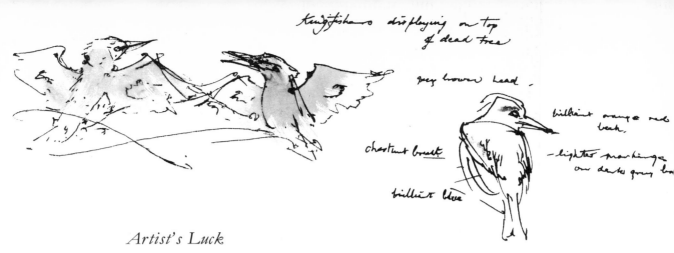

kingfishers displaying on top
of dead tree

grey brown head.

brilliant orange red
beak.

chestnut breast

lighter markings
on darker grey b...

brilliant blue

Artist's Luck

Often, while I was sitting quietly sketching one subject, something else would pop up unexpectedly. This happened late one morning, when we had turned off the road to find a position from which to sketch a pair of baobab trees that had taken my fancy.

I had scarcely started to draw before a grey headed kingfisher flew into a nearby bush and sat there, scrutinising the ground below. These kingfishers have adapted themselves to 'fishing' for insects and grubs on the ground, using the same technique as when fishing in a stream. Evidently it saw nothing of interest and soon it started to preen, pausing every now and then to look about, giving me a fine opportunity to record its characteristic postures.

A quick movement in the same scrubby thorn sent the kingfisher winging off towards the lake and a small darkish olive-grey squirrel ran up the tree. This little bush squirrel lay along a branch, hoping perhaps that it had not been seen, but then came close to have a good look at us.

While I was busy sketching my new model, Martin kept a sharp eye on the immediate vicinity. He pointed out a large grey shape on a branch high up in an acacia thorn about fifty yards away. It was a Verreaux's eagle owl. By raising the car window to the exact height to take the weight of a powerful pair of binoculars, I could examine the ear tufts and the dark markings round the eye disks, and then make quick sketches. The owl was watching us with his eyes half open; sometimes one eye would close altogether, showing clearly the extraordinary powder-pink eyelids. Presently he turned his back on us, but now and then his head suddenly swivelled round, eyes staring at us to see if the intruders were still on his territory. I never completed my sketch of the baobab trees but returned more than satisfied with the morning's work.

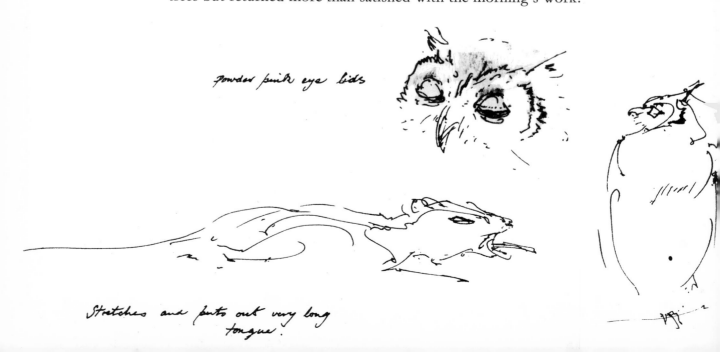

powder pink eye lids

Stretches and puts out very long
tongue.

little streams running down
through rocks along road
spreading out through reeds
below

baby

baby in young tree
with large round
ears

goes off into
reeds with baby
clinging under
body.

baby in pick-a-back
position

Large troupe of baboon all round us
sykes monkeys and hornbill in trees

on top of 'chimney' of termite hill.

Bushbuck
ram

baby in mothers arms.

Bushbuck steps daintily
down road followed by young baboon

grooming
mother cleaning babies toes.

...shbuck slipping in and out of cover —
— noise — bustle — rapidly changing scene.

baby baboon

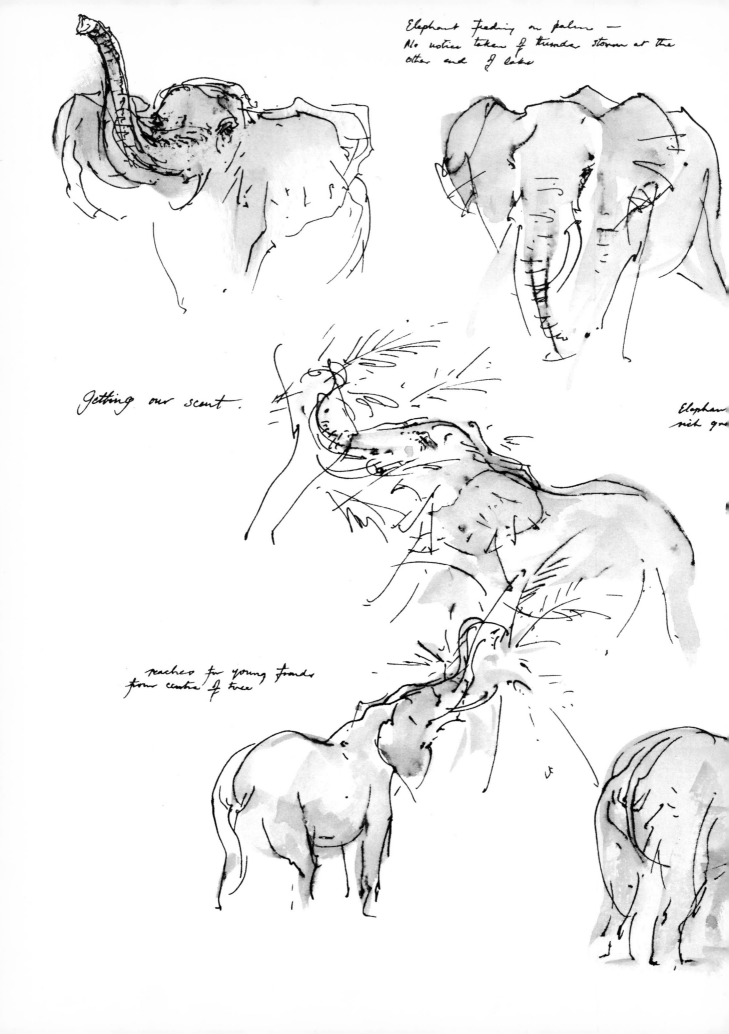

Elephant feeding on palms —
No notice taken of thunder storm at the
other end of lake

Getting our scent.

Elephant
rich gr...

reaches for young fronds
from centre of tree

grey against
palm

approaches with head bobbing and rocking
from side to side

off carrying palm frond
in tip of trunk

pillar box red
around eye   and wat[t]

White primaries

A pair of ground hornbill - about 50 yds away in tussocky grass
at foot of thorn tree. One of them catches small snake -
about 2½ ft long. Snaps at it with bill, bashes it on ground.
Snake trails along from the bill quite limp - disappears head first.
Hornbill apparently unconcerned by the whole operation.

throat .

loop of snake sticking out from side of hill.

Snake - pale olive green to grey .

Tiger snake ?

violet grey of escarpment

varying darks of trees

sundrenched gold of dried grass.

resting position

contrast blue grey of thundery sky with
luminous gold of grass

grey
termite hill.

washing   washing

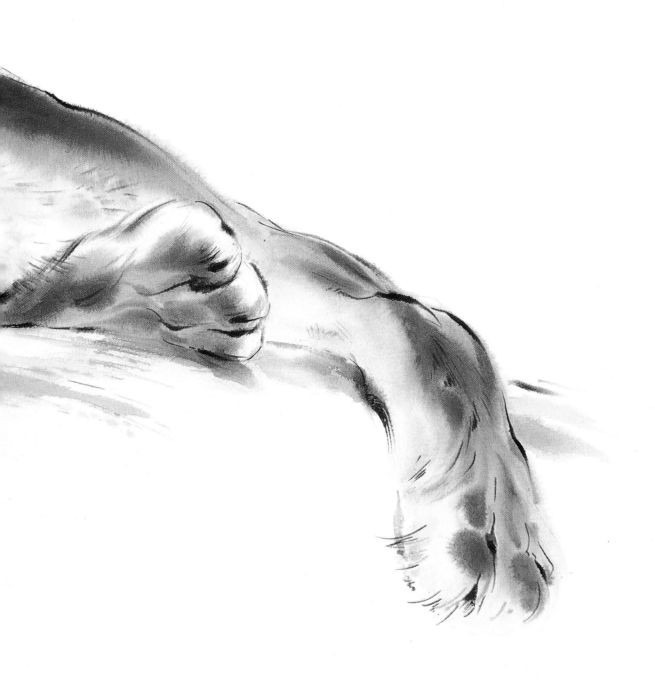

Saddle billed
stork

Black-headed heron

a pair of Goliath heron in middle distance

Spoonbill

Stilt -

geese?

Pelicans preening

tones and colours shimmer in brilliant light.

bewildering contrasts in scale - from the pelicans - storks
and herons down to the smallest of the waders - the little stint.

buffalo - egret - oxpeckers.

blue black storm cloud

Fever trees and egrets brilliant against gloomy background.

(approx 500 buffalo – ½ doz zebra in foreground)

mock battle between two males
— egret move a few yards away and wait
until it is over.

Impala washing themselves after storm

Lake Manyara   16th Oct

oxpeckers on impala

oxpecker at nostril

red-billed oxpeckers.

egret

1.

2.

Sudden alert at approach of a pair of Warthog.

3.

4.

Trial of strength between two male impalas
ending in wild chase round the clearing
in the forest – watched by the rest of
the herd of males.

Lake Manyara   15th Oct.

Lions in Trees

The lions of Lake Manyara are famous for their habit of climbing and resting in trees. One does not usually have the chance to watch a lion scaling a tree trunk or lounging amongst the branches at some height above the ground. New themes present a challenge to the artist. It is not only a question of studying the unfamiliar movements and positions of an animal, it is also the fact that the animal itself makes a fresh impact.

It seems that once lions have established the habit of climbing trees they continue to do so regularly in the same locality. In the Lake Manyara area they are usually to be found in *Acacia tortilis*. To the visitor it is at once obvious that this thorn tree, with its short stout trunk and angled branches, is easily climbed. The reason why lions climb trees is not so obvious and various explanations have been put forward. It is possible that at some height from the ground the breeze is cooler and there is some relief from the troublesome attentions of tsetse flies. It may also be that a tree provides a good vantage point. Whatever the reasons, my task was to concentrate on my new visual problems of anatomy and perspective, and, above all, to see these splendid beasts with a new awareness.

On our first afternoon in the park we found a fine black-maned lion high up in a thorn tree, using the tortuous spread of the branches just below the crown as a mattress. He was so high up and well hidden by the network of twigs and branches that it was not until I was right under the tree that I could make him out at all. He scarcely bothered to glance at the two cars below, but every so often raised himself to look far into the distance. Although he shifted his position quite often, as though he were a bit uncomfortable, easing a limb or rolling his great belly on to a smoother part of the branch, I got the definite impression that he very much liked being up there.

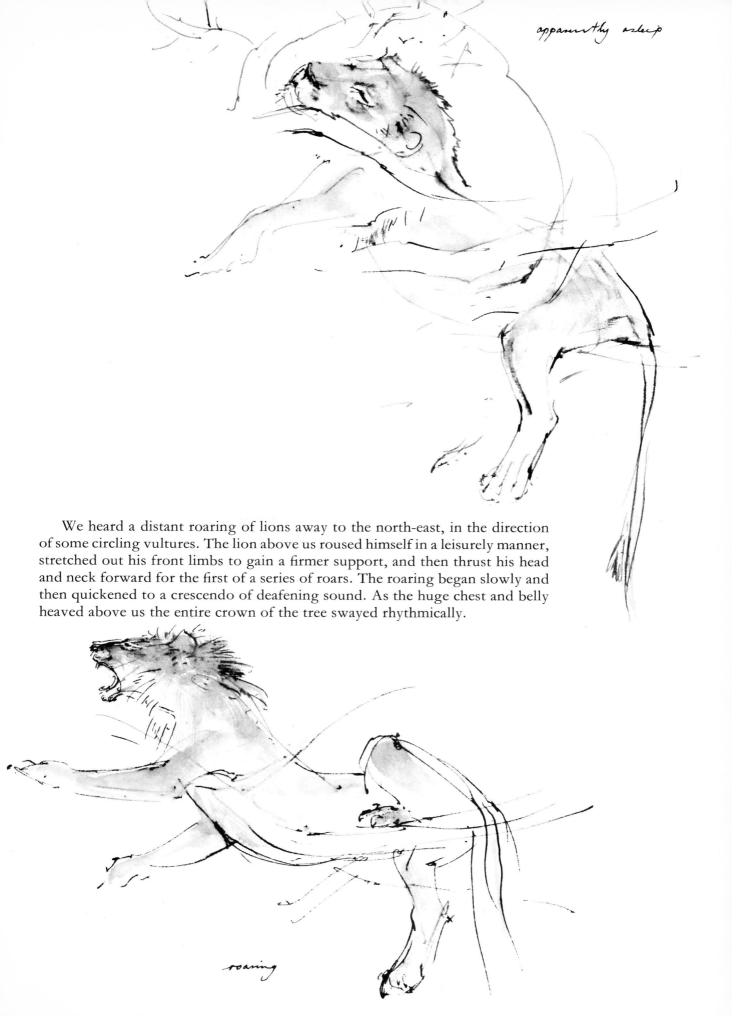

apparently asleep

We heard a distant roaring of lions away to the north-east, in the direction of some circling vultures. The lion above us roused himself in a leisurely manner, stretched out his front limbs to gain a firmer support, and then thrust his head and neck forward for the first of a series of roars. The roaring began slowly and then quickened to a crescendo of deafening sound. As the huge chest and belly heaved above us the entire crown of the tree swayed rhythmically.

roaring

Crowned crane landing
Striking pattern of black and white against sky

Part of herd of about 60 elephant moving through long grass near lake.

scale - baby to mother.

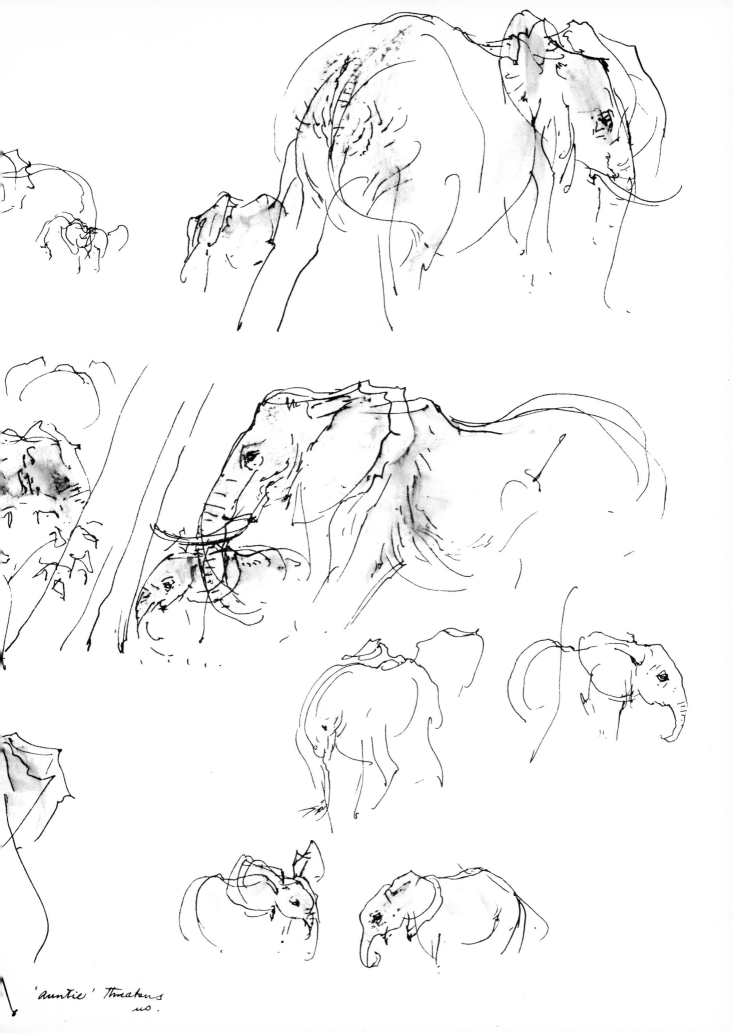

'auntie' threatens
us.

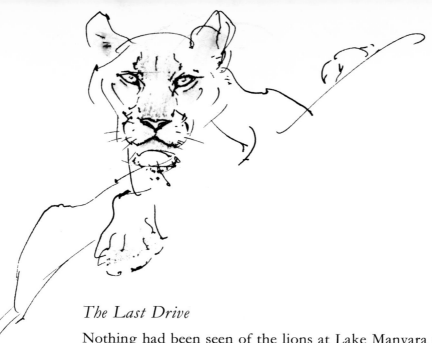

The Last Drive

Nothing had been seen of the lions at Lake Manyara since our first afternoon. The park guides said that we were very unlucky, but that the very dry weather might have something to do with their absence. We often heard them, but the only indication of their whereabouts was the circling of vultures in an inaccessible part of the park at the foot of the escarpment.

At the park gate on the last afternoon of my stay I heard a report that a lioness had been seen that morning. Under the directions of Zacharias, one of the park guides, we drove deep into the park and cruised about under spreading acacia thorns. In a short time we found what we were searching for. The sad remains of an impala lay hidden under a thick bush, and a lioness lay on her back in the grass, eyes closed and paws dangling in the air limply, then she flopped over onto her side. Half an hour later, a ring of cars surrounded the lioness while she, thoroughly replete, took not the slightest notice.

Fortunately for me, photographs take much less time than drawings, and the other cars left one by one. Presently the lioness sat up. She gave us a look which seemed to go through us rather than at us, then rose to her feet and disappeared round some thick bushes.

I assumed that this would be the end of the session but Zacharias spoke quickly to Martin who at once started the car. We turned and followed the tracks of the other cars back to the nearest road and then, after a few minutes of rapid driving, we left the road and came to a halt on a bank overlooking a gulley. Below us was the lioness crouching beside a stream. We arrived just as she was raising her head from the water. She went up the bank, walked slowly towards a big acacia thorn tree and then climbed effortlessly up the sloping trunk on to a low branch. There she stood watching us for a moment. In a fork about twenty-five feet from the ground, she finally flopped down on a thick limb of the tree. The light was fading, so we drove a little closer and then, as she kept her head turned away, Martin drove on under the tree in order to get a better view.

The rules of the park specify that all visitors must leave well before dusk. It was already getting late and there was only time for me to put down a few stark outlines; then, just as we were about to go, the lioness got up and I had some lovely glimpses of her climbing confidently about among the spreading branches. Finally she slipped head first down the bole of the tree and disappeared. We made as speedy a journey back towards the park entrance as we could. On the way, we passed the smallest baby elephant of any that we had seen but there was no time to stop.

We reached a point on the one road out of the park which earlier in the day had been blocked by a big tree that had fallen across it, making a small detour necessary. All day the staff had worked hard to get the road clear. Now it was completely blocked again, this time by a herd of elephants, about fifty strong, feasting on the fresh green of the leaves.

Martin stopped the car and looked at Zacharias. They talked it over for a moment and then Martin turned down the rough track of the detour, through thickets of tough saplings with just sufficient room for a car to pass. As Martin eased the car slowly over the bumpy ground, skirting the torn roots of the fallen tree to climb up the slope towards the road again, we found our escape blocked by one of the big 'Aunties' of the herd standing sideways across the track. Her head swung slowly round towards us. It was a tense moment. I found that I did not feel afraid, just very alert and curious to know how it would end. Zacharias had his head out of the window sizing up the mood of the elephant. Then he started talking to 'Auntie' in Swahili and presently she shambled sideways up the trail and out on to the road. The car moved forward again only to find another enormous female with ears spread wide and a baby on each side of her, towering above us. I do not know what Zacharias said to her but she made no fuss as Martin quickly drove the car past her. Soon we were hurrying through the darkening forest towards the park gate.

Serengeti National Park

Tanzania

On the road to the Serengeti from Ngorongoro.

The Drive to the Ngorongoro Crater and the Serengeti

We left Lake Manyara behind and drove up the escarpment and over the rolling hills of the Mbulu plateau. We travelled for half an hour through this dry, arid plateau and then, in the distance, we saw the long line of the Ngorongoro crater. At the foot of the crater the land became more fertile and we passed through stretches of ripening wheat and coffee plantations. We climbed steeply for some time and then looking back caught glimpses of the landscape below through the moss-draped trees of the rain forest. High up on the side of the crater, the road traversed a gorge, dense with giant trees. Higher still, the trees became smaller, the patches of sunlight larger, and in a few minutes we were at the top looking out over a spectacular view. As an artist, I found it too vast and overwhelming to tempt me to work; none the less it held me entranced by the luminous distances and I found myself absorbed in trying to come to some sort of visual understanding of its scale.

There is a lodge at the rim of the crater. Here we sat and drank coffee leisurely while looking down, some two thousand feet, on to the floor of the crater. I began to pick out some tiny dots below and identify individual animals with the binoculars. Buffalo, zebra and wildebeest were comparatively easy to distinguish. On the lake, minute specks turned out to be a flock of pelicans and we were able to make out the occasional heron. Large numbers of smaller birds proved too difficult to identify. After leaving the lodge, we stopped at each vantage point to watch the play of light and shade over the crater. Then we turned away down the Olbalbal escarpment in the direction of the Serengeti. I had half expected another belt of dense forest; instead, we found an open sun-drenched landscape, stretching away into the distance, a sky decorated with buoyant clouds and the

Grant's gazelle 'robertsi'

long perspectives accentuated by cloud shadows. There were no coffee plantations, no wheatfields, no cultivation of any kind, only endless open grassland.
Zebra and Masai cattle were dotted about the plain and sometimes grazing close
together. There were 'manyatta', the thorn-enclosed camps of Masai about a
couple of hundred yards from the road and fitting perfectly into the landscape.

As we dropped gently down into the plain we saw small herds of 'Tommies'—
Thomson's gazelle—and a variety of Grant's gazelle (*robertsi*), with horns of a
much more open shape, as if some strong hand had forced them apart. We
stopped to watch the occasional secretary bird pacing the grass as it hunted for
reptiles, insects, or young birds and for the first time we were able to watch the
handsome Kori bustard at close quarters. One of these dignified looking birds
was keeping company with a silver-backed jackal and was obviously quite
capable of looking after himself.

When I find background that interests me, I can pose a cheetah or group of
antelope against it in my mind's eye to see how it would look in a painting. We
broke the journey several times while I admired the magnificent structural
counterpoint of differing thorn trees or examined a new flower or plant.

Thomson's gazelle

After a week of looking at the African scene from a car window I was glad to put my feet on the earth again. On one occasion while crouching to study a plant I heard a slight movement. I looked up to find two ancient Masai women, one at each side of me. They had materialised quite silently but now broke into a noisy stream of Swahili, while, to my alarm, long bony fingers began flickering all over me. The women were loosely clad in the earth-red robes of the Masai and my confusion was not lessened when I found long shrivelled breasts dangling inches away from my nose. Struggling frantically to my feet, I bolted for the car with the two old crones still clinging to me. I could not imagine why they were so menacing. As I crept into the haven of the car there was a loud altercation between Martin and the women before he slid the car forward leaving them looking quite incredulous. He was shaking with laughter as he explained that it was neither money nor my life they were after but merely cigarettes—and none of us smoked. While I was pulling myself together and making sure I was still intact, Martin continued to shake with mirth. The event had obviously made his day. Frankly, one of the so-called fiercer animals would have scared me far less.

Kori bustard with
Jackal only a few yards
away

orange head.
robult hues on tail

agama lizard.

Detail of Kopje near Seronera Lodge

Dik dik

Sea of Grass

The plain of the Serengeti seems to me like a sea of grass, so flat that the car seems to float over it without any need of a road. A high wind playing through the grass keeps it in constant motion, creating the waves of this golden sea. The sound of the car brushing through the grass, the play of the wind through the windows, the eye just high enough to spot a secretary bird, but low enough to feel part of the sun-bleached waving landscape—all this had the exhilaration of sailing along in a small boat.

The occasional areas of acacia woodland accentuate the feeling of immense space and freedom of movement. But when we crossed a stretch where the grass was grazed to a worn stubble, the magic disappeared. In spite of the thin green blades of new grass peeping through everywhere, I found myself hating the sordid look of bare earth and longing to get back into the constantly changing shapes and shadows of the tall grass. Depending on the time of day, the colour changed from silver grey, tinged with violet, to the deep gold of a ripe corn field. It was always the same and yet always different.

Rugged islands of granite pierced the horizontal planes of gold. Giant boulders, rounded and sculpted so that the eye plays over each shoulder of rock, reminded me of those Japanese gardens where carefully chosen rocks are arranged in a flat area of sand. The weathering of the stone, the pattern of lichens, the runnels and stains, all accentuate the rounded forms. Known as 'kopjes', these outcrops of rock provide shade and conserve moisture. They vary in size but each one provides a pocket of shelter, food and shade for forms of life that could not survive for long in the open plains. Trees and shrubs cluster around them, softening the starkness of the rock and incidentally providing a habitat for a variety of small animals, the most conspicuous of which are the rock hyrax.

Rock hyrax – Seronera

Near the lodge at Seronera, which is happily situated in the shelter of a group of kopjes, the rock hyraxes have become remarkably bold. They cadge titbits from the kitchen and I found that they were prepared to come within a few yards of me, thus making them easy models to draw.

The Tree and the Rock Hyrax are the animals referred to in the Bible as Coneys. They are about the same size and have the general appearance of rabbits, though with a more stocky build and with much smaller ears. The most extraordinary feature about them is that each toe carries a little hoof. And the unique structure of their padded feet gives them a suction hold on a vertical surface, so that both are good jumpers and climbers. Evidently, their tooth structure is also of special interest to the zoologist, as it is close to that of a rhinoceros. I believe they now stand in a group of their own but with the elephant as their closest relative.

Looking out from our room in the lodge we could nearly always see a herd of Thomson's gazelle and the occasional giraffe or buffalo. We became familiar with the call of the go-away bird and the duets of D'Arnand's barbets around the lodge.

At night bats fluttered a few feet away from the lamps on the veranda, hunting for their supper. Once a mysterious humped shape moved out in the moonlight which we took to be a honey badger. The nights are very still for the wind drops at sunset, but the silence is shattered by the bark of an occasional jackal and most hauntingly by the hyenas calling to each other. These eerie cries were so much a part of the nights in the Serengeti that we became accustomed to them.

But sometimes they would wake us just before dawn and we roused ourselves to watch the pale greenish gold of the sky deepen to a rich orange red. The finely pointed detail of a few ragged thorn trees made a magical silhouette as steely tips took on the texture of soft black velvet.

Walking away with severed head

A pair of lioness on kill – a Topi.
A third waits her turn a few yds away
but is driven off by one of the others.
One is asleep having eaten her fill.

Black-headed heron.

Stopped to make sketch — as it paced v. slowly through long grass. Saw it make sudden strike. It raised head with small rat in it's beak. Shrill squeaking subsided as heron shook it and tightened grip on neck.

heron stepping very slowly through
tall grass

Sudden gulp — rat disappears head first lump moved very slowly down neck

Topi

Leopards

In the Serengeti I had many opportunities to draw leopards but our first sight of them was the most memorable. Three topi antelopes were standing together facing towards a 'dongo' or gully. We drove closer and found a female leopard and her cub picking their way among the tall dried-up stems of plants and scrubby thorns along the bottom of the gully. They were so well concealed that but for the topi we would never have discovered them. Now and then, they broke into a loping run, a dazzling rhythm of tawny gold, with black markings flashing strongly on the white fur under their bodies.

Suddenly the mother went ahead with tail held high in the air. The cub sat down for a moment watching her, then followed the clear black and white signal of the tip of her tail which waved above the brown plants of the gully. The leopardess climbed a tree and settled herself to gaze out over the plain. We had lost sight of the cub; we felt sure it must be somewhere within sight of the tree, but when we searched, it was too skilfully hidden to be found, at any rate from the car.

During the next few days we often looked for this mother and cub but without success, though once in the same area, we thought we recognised the mother high up in a tree. We stayed very still. Twenty minutes later she leaped lightly down and settled herself in the grass below. By slow degrees, Martin edged the car closer until I could make sketches of her outside the car window.

cub following leopardess.

cub half hidden in grass

Tail held very high
as she went
down gully.

leopardess climbs tree
leaving cubs hidden in "dongo"

leopard studies - Serengeti - 18th Oct.

Tawny and Bataleur eagles sitting side
by side on branch.

Tawny eagle

crest rises
when alarmed

Hyena —
Far side of jowl clotted with blood

Slender Mongoose

Tail pos. as it ran in front of us

Hyena at foot of tree
all heads raised as we
approached

Tail pattern of secretary bird in flight

Banded Mongoose

running through grass.

Crested Hawk Eagle.

Crowned plover chicks

Sec. bird seen through veil of grass.

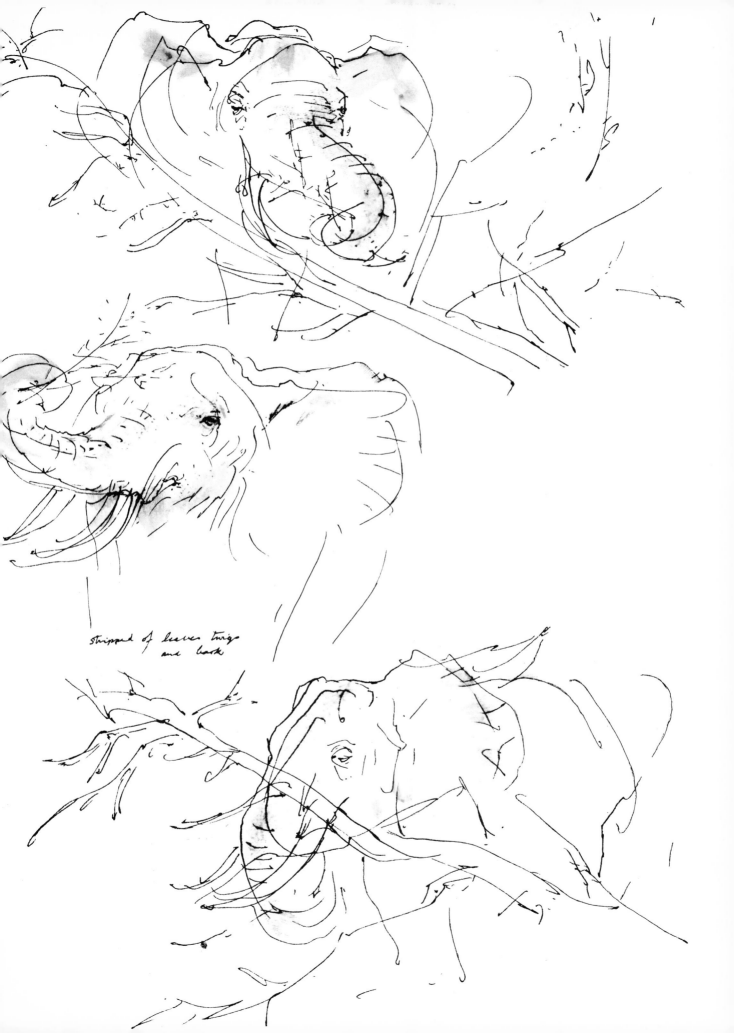

stripped of leaves twigs
and bark

A pair of black-maned lions.

Lionesses and cubs

Cheetahs in the Serengeti

We came upon our first group of cheetahs in the late afternoon. Two well-grown youngsters and an adult female, which we assumed was their mother, were resting together in short grass. We watched them for an hour or so while I sketched the group in various poses. Suddenly as if at a given signal, the mother got up and walked away. She never looked back, and we lost sight of her as she merged into the pale gold of the middle distance.

In the days that followed, we saw the youngsters quite often, but they were always alone. It is just possible that we witnessed the moment when the mother finally left her cubs to their own devices. If this were so, then from now on, they would have to fend for themselves.

Standing at the door of our room early one morning, we had a grandstand view of our two young cheetahs on the hunt. They were stalking a herd of 'Tommies' making a very slow approach with heads held well down below the level of their shoulders. Every so often they stood stock still for a few minutes, 'frozen' in their tracks, before making another short stealthy run. Inching their way forward, they gradually closed the distance between them and the herd.

From where we stood it was clear that the cheetahs, keeping station with each other some sixty paces apart, were concentrating on one particular gazelle that was feeding at a little distance from the others. To us the cheetahs looked so conspicuous that it was difficult to believe that the herd of 'Tommies' could possibly be unaware of the danger and yet the gazelles gave no sign of nervousness. The suspense was almost unbearable as the cheetahs succeeded in halving the distance, to come within possible range for the final burst of speed that should end in a kill.

And then everything happened at once; I saw several gazelles raise their heads, break away and set the whole herd in motion. At the same time the cheetahs raced to head off their quarry but the lone gazelle moved at tremendous speed and soon regained the safety of the fleeing herd. The chaos was short but spectacular. The disappointed cheetahs quickly gave up, turned and walked slowly away from the herd, finally flopping down, side by side, in a clump of short grass. The herd then stopped and every head turned towards the spot where the cheetahs lay.

We were inclined to think that the inexperience of the cheetahs had made them too eager and that they had started the final burst of speed too soon, or they may have betrayed their presence by some hasty movement, thereby giving the prey that vital extra second to escape. Later the same day, about a mile away, we found the evidence of what may well have been their first successful hunt together. The remains of a caracase lay at the foot of a tree which we passed on our way back to the Lodge at sunset. The head of the dead gazelle was undamaged and still looked strangely beautiful.

Whenever we met this pair of cheetahs they were always within a few miles of the Lodge and they never showed any sign of fear in our presence. They would come forward to lie down in the shade of the car, one of them sometimes even using us as a lookout post, the two front paws resting on the boot or front bumper while the cheetah stretched to its full height and took stock of the surroundings.

Black shouldered kite

After several attempts our guide found another group of cheetahs for us, a mother with two cubs. The cubs must have been about seven or eight weeks old, the white mane of the baby cheetah still showing from the crown of the head to the base of the tail. At this age the cubs look half-cheetah, half-monkey. They were a little way off, half hidden in a clump of grass.

The mother walked slowly over to a termite heap and sat there, looking out over the plain towards a large herd of 'Tommies' and Grant's gazelle. The cubs then joined her. After a while the mother moved off and we saw that she was heading towards the stragglers of the herd. The cubs followed a little way and then sat down. The pattern of the early morning hunt was repeated: the same lowered head and neck disguising the typical rangy silhouette of a cheetah, the same slow closing of the gap between the hunter and the one gazelle selected for attack. This hunt too was unsuccessful and, once again, the cheetah broke it off the moment she saw she had been spotted, while the herd lined up at a safe distance watching the cheetah as she walked slowly back to her cubs.

The same evening we were given an eye-witness account of how the mother had made a kill late that afternoon. After a slow approach upwind, the mother cheetah succeeded in launching her attack before the startled 'Tommy' sensed the danger. Perhaps some trick of evening light enabled her to get close enough before unleashing her final burst of speed. The gazelle took flight but was quickly overtaken, seized by the throat and within seconds all was over. The cheetah threw herself down beside the dead 'Tommy' and lay there panting. She then sat up very erect and, curling back her lips to reveal her teeth, she uttered a thin high-pitched cry. The cubs immediately left their clump of grass and raced towards her. While the mother lay resting nearby, the cubs leaped about

20ᵗʰ Oct.

over the body of the dead gazelle. When they looked as though they were determined to get at the meat, the mother got up and fell to work on the carcase. The feast began.

Being squeamish by nature, I take comfort from the fact that human beings who have been mauled by lion or leopard report no sensation of pain. Evidently the nature of the blows stun and numb the victim. A fortnight later this was confirmed by a conversation with a hunter, who told us that although his fore-arm was slashed and his scalp grazed in a sudden attack by a leopard, at the time he had experienced no pain, only the dull weight of the blows.

Wild gardenia -

'Gardenia jovis tonantis'
   — or Jove's Thunderbolt Tree

Masai Mara Game Reserve

Kenya

Keekerok Lodge

Seen in the hot sunshine of late October, with an occasional storm cloud gathering, the Masai Mara gave an impression of rugged vitality and of rough wide open spaces. The land itself looks tougher, more barren, the trees more ragged than in the Serengeti. The eye scans mile after mile of undulating ground covered with grass and scrubby thorn; in the middle distance are patches of the darker green of woodland in among the stretches of gold. Far away on the horizon are the outlines of hills and mountains.

In the Masai Mara reserve we found some of the huge herds of game which had migrated northwards from the Serengeti. Sometimes a black line standing out from the mellow greys and golds made us raise our binoculars and we saw a thousand buffalo or more. Although the herds were often grazing peacefully, I was left with a vivid impression of everything being on the move, as if something in the atmosphere was keeping all the animals alert. This impression was especially strong near Keekerok Lodge where there were large numbers of wildebeest and zebra. The wildebeest, in particular, careered about for no apparent reason, galloping without even appearing to look where they were going. The zebra sometimes joined in, completing the sense of exuberant vitality.

Keekerok Lodge has been built in a gentle hollow sheltered by tall and gracefully spreading acacia thorns. The grass in front of the guest rooms is watered by a sprinkler during the day and cropped short by zebra and waterbuck at night. Elephants, giraffe and waterbuck, wildebeest, zebra and topi are frequent visitors

Vervet monkeys raiding the bird table. Keekerok 22^d Oct.

to a dam which has been constructed in full view of the lodge. The camp scavengers, a flock of marabou storks about fifty strong, often group themselves there in macabre elegance. They have built big untidy nests of twigs in the flat top of a tall acacia thorn, overlooking the refuse dump at the back of the lodge. The moment a truck arrives with a fresh load of refuse from the kitchen, they spiral slowly down to pick it over for tit-bits before the remains are burnt.

The acrobats and chief entertainers around the lodge are the agile vervet monkeys; the villains are three massive old buffalo bulls, nicknamed 'The three old men of Keekerok'. There are prides of lions in the neighbourhood, and one has the impression that the other animals gain a certain sense of security when near the lodge. Even so, a topi was killed by a lion within a hundred yards of the lodge during the few days that we were there.

Night after night we were woken by a steady but resonant sound of munching. In bright moonlight we watched a herd of zebra cropping the grass just outside our windows. Standing by the plate-glass screen which separated our room from a low-tiled veranda, we could see the zebras tirelessly and rhythmically tearing at the crisp stalks and crunching them up, only raising their heads an inch or two for an occasional shake or snuffle. Close to us a very young foal stood perfectly still. There was something toy-like about him, as he stood on his long legs as if on tiptoes, and something unreal, as if he half remembered some other world and didn't yet belong to this one.

fish eagle

marabout storks and nests

Dikdik in grasses
at foot of Masai Kopje —
looking minute against giant boulders
low sun — rich burnished colour.

Zebra in high spirits

Distant herds — zebra — wildebeest — buffalo.

Wildebeest

Keekrok 21st oct

Nubian Vulture's nest

lilac-breasted roller
Thompson's gazelle

Buffalo skull

The three old male buffalo near the lodge

Buffa

Impala

arges the car

Keekerok   21st Oct

A Strange Incident

Driving back towards the lodge one evening around sunset we found three cars drawn up at the side of the road. They appeared to be watching a group of antelopes: four topi with two calves. Martin then spotted something at the foot of a tree about eighty yards behind the topi. At first we took this to be a lion but with binoculars we identified it as a large hyena. Someone in another car pointed out a tawny shape sixty paces to the right of the topi. It was a leopard. The topi nearest it, a handsome male, appeared to be looking directly at the leopard while the others looked uneasily about them. Then the topi, in a straggling line with the male in the lead, calves in the middle and another adult bringing up the rear, started slowly towards the leopard as if completely unaware of the danger.

At once the leopard flattened itself among the grasses. It was not easy to judge the distance between hunter and hunted and we held our breath as the procession drew level with the leopard. But the topi passed safely by, and the last adult in the line turned on the leopard with lowered horns. The leopard rose slowly, stood its ground for a moment and then, with a few angry swipes of the tail, made off towards the tree. The hyena also got to its feet and for a moment or two the leopard and the hyena faced each other sullenly with the bole of the tree between them. The hyena looked the larger and more powerful beast, and stood its ground. The leopard was having a bad evening, and for the second time I watched its long tail sweeping through the air. Then with a couple of bounds and a splendid leap, it draped itself gracefully over the limb of a small bent tree nearby.

Leopard - drawn from
Major Temple Boreham's
landrover

Oct 22ⁿ

Vervet Monkeys

During the day, at Keekerok, my wife 'Bill' could watch vervet monkeys on a tree beyond the veranda. Soon she made friends with them by offering them bits of our few remaining bananas, being very careful to keep well out of range of a bad-tempered old male. The vervets became accustomed to playing just outside the plate-glass window and I was fascinated by their antics during the afternoon siesta. About a dozen light-footed monkeys leaped about in complete abandon, within a few feet of me, making spectacular entrances and exits like some enthusiastic but quite unrehearsed corps de ballet.

For an artist who is sketching animals in the wild, one of the many problems is how to get close enough to his subject. The vervet monkeys were in an ideal situation and the plate-glass screen kept them at the right distance from me. Their black faces, ruffed with white fur, were close enough to see the detail; their torsos and limbs were so near that I experienced the sense of touch, that feeling of running one's hand over the form which is so important for drawing. At the same time, they were careering about with an uninhibited zest for life which even the best of zoos cannot produce.

My difficulty was that there were too many models and far too much going on. The constant interplay of movement in a dozen or so very lively monkeys made it almost impossible to concentrate on any one of them. I had to snatch at every opportunity to grasp the essentials of an arresting pose, or to put down detailed information of a head or paw.

A Distraction Display

At Keekerok, we went on several expeditions with Major Temple-Boreham (who, until his death in May 1969, was senior game warden, Narok District, and was known throughout the world for his lifetime of service to the preservation of wild life). One morning, he spotted a pair of ostrich with chicks in a patch of whistling thorn. We left the road, and the landrover zig-zagged towards them over bumpy ground in and out of the thorn scrub. The chicks moved along in compact formation, heads up, legs twinkling below the mottled plumage which camouflages them so well. They were so close together that they looked like some enormous woolly centipede charging through the grass.

The female led us away from her chicks at once, making sure of our attention by fluttering the huge flight feathers of one wing, as though she had just broken it. She scarcely seemed able to drag it along, but a moment later that wing was flapping healthily and the other started dragging at an alarming angle. 'T.B.' stopped the landrover long enough for me to try to put it down on paper but the result was quite chaotic. We caught up with her again and she gave us a repeat performance, then she assumed a low Groucho Marx gait and for a few moments appeared on the point of collapse. With a great effort, she put on a burst of speed with wings flapping wildly, then she faltered, staggered a few paces and fell down, nothing but a pathetic heap of feathers, wings awry, head lifted a little and gasping painfully. We slowed down and then stopped to make a sketch but she was up and away with beautifully coordinated strides, making tremendous speed. In spite of all this effort, and after beguiling us away to what she felt was a safe distance, she then led us straight back to her chicks.

gasping —
lower mandible
moves up and down
loose skin below it
flaps about.

'Groucho Marx' stride - wings flapping - undulating.
- broken wings - broken leg - finally, pathetic
collapse -

chicks pelting along - raising miniature dust cloud

Jefassa's Waterbuck

Kukenth

Eland

A dozen male eland - alerted by our car
charge about leaping and bucking.
a giraffe picks up their mood and joins them
at a distance.

½ mile away a large herd of eland with young - about 100.
very lively - make off until out of range of binoculars

a frieze of giraffe   Keekush.

white side whiskers
already v. pronounced

Warthog sow with
babies.

Group of five Oribi among rocks and scrub
on high ground near Mara river
white shows strongly on rump, under belly or
on front of chest.

The Spring-haas

The spring-haas or spring hare is entirely nocturnal. It is about the size of a rabbit, with a handsome black tip to the tail and, but for its ears, has a squirrel-like appearance, especially when it tucks up its very short front legs under its chin as it sits up. The long powerful back legs and its manner of covering the ground in long hops remind one of a kangaroo. Keekerok seemed a likely place to find this creature which had delighted me so often in the zoo, but the days slipped by and on the drives after dark in Major Temple-Boreham's landrover we had so far failed to discover one.

One night, just as we were about to turn in, there was a knock at our door and Martin appeared. While taking a message from one part of the camp to another, he had found a spring-haas. We obtained permission to use the car for

switches direction
Sweeps and turns
ears erect — tail arched

fur fluffs out — tail arches
as he chases jackal away — nearly catches him by the tail.

ears forward

undulation of body - particularly of tail - adjusting to the powerful hopping movement

sketching and very soon we picked up a brilliant point of light gleaming and dancing about ahead of us, and then vanishing. Martin's approach was most skilful: he drove a little to one side of the point of light, as if to pass it by, then turned so that the headlights were directed on to the animal. For a few moments there was a clear impression of shape and proportion and I began to sketch but while I was putting down the first few lines, the spring-haas bounded away. We spent an hour patiently dodging between trees and a line of rondevals (or round thatched huts) with Martin trying to keep my model sufficiently in view to creep up once more and catch it in the beam of the headlights. The session ended when I took too long over a sketch and we lost our spring-haas for good.

Hyena puppies — long shaggy coat
black 'stockings'
spots still very faint

Bat-eared Foxes and Hyena Puppies

One evening, soon after dark, we drove off in the landrover to look for bat-eared foxes. These charming little nocturnal creatures are often seen sitting about near their burrows in the daytime during the rainy seasons but they are much more difficult to find in the dry conditions of October. I had searched for them without success in the Nairobi Park and around Seronera. But a mile or two from Keekerok lodge we managed to locate a pair on the airstrip, though all I could see was two little grey shapes running away in front of the headlamps.

Returning to camp, we stopped by a culvert to watch a jackal and hyena ahead of us. Then up from the culvert into the beam of our lights, scrambled a pair of oddly proportioned creatures. They could only be hyena puppies. Apart from an occasional glance, they took no notice of us. I made a few sketches, but before I could finish, they tumbled backwards into the ditch out of sight.

To my great satisfaction, we found the bat-eared foxes again early next morning, on the same bit of open grass near the airstrip. They appeared to be rather nervous of the landrover but I was able to make a few studies.

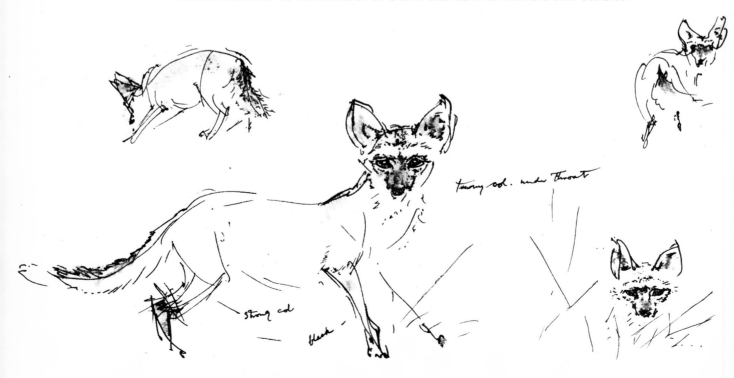

Secretary bird killing a snake

A Wet Afternoon

Major Temple-Boreham was very insistent that we must go out with him on our one wet afternoon. He assured us that the rain would make the animals much more lively, and he ordered his two scouts to take guns in the landrover with us just in case of trouble.

We passed another ostrich family and again watched a short distraction display, but we moved on because the scouts were looking for rhino which the Major thought 'might be interesting'. Eventually we found two. They were sitting close together in a patch of mud, their bulky armoured bodies no longer grey, but glistening black in the rain. Their ears pricked at the sound of the engine. First one got to its feet to inspect the approaching green landrover and then the other. 'Now I shall go very close,' said T.B. 'But don't worry.' They faced us indecisively for a few moments, then one collapsed back into the mud as if it had been shot, while the other proceeded to lumber around it in circles. 'They have evidently decided that we are too big an animal,' said T.B. 'They don't know what to do about it, so they are letting off steam.'

Their movements were very similar to the quick bouncing and jostling of piglets and they had the same way of suddenly stopping quite motionless to stare at us. The smaller of the two was particularly skittish. Its massive, awkward-looking body frisked about, swinging first one way and then the other, while flinging its cumbersome head up and down. Every now and then it leaped clear of the ground, jerked itself around in mid-air and landed facing in another direction. No animal artist could ever invent a rhino dancing in the rain, and having seen it, he would probably be very unwise ever to attempt to paint it.

Rhino family against skyline   Oct 22ⁿᵈ

Dancing in the rain

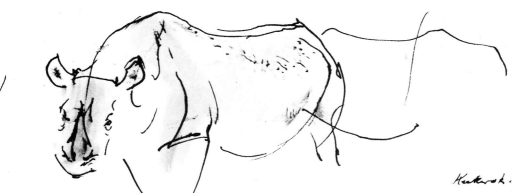

Kuskush.   24ᵗʰ Oct

Lions

Late in the same afternoon we came upon a big blond lion sitting on a bare patch of ground encircled by whistling thorns. After a time the lion got up, strode across to the nearest tree and pushed his great head and neck slowly backwards and forwards under one of its spiky branches, as if combing his mane. Every few minutes he stopped to roar. The roars echoed and throbbed then dwindled into silence but there was no answering roar.

Not long after we had moved off the scouts spotted two black-maned lions on sloping ground about half a mile away. Ten minutes later, we came upon a group of three lionesses with nine cubs. We approached very slowly and soon they were all round the landrover, lying spread out in groups of twos and threes. The light was fading quickly and I started sketching at once. Suddenly we noticed all their heads turn in one direction. Appearing over the shoulder of the gentle slope below us was a lioness followed by another and yet another. Then we saw movements in the grass around them and in a few minutes, our first party was joined by this second group of three lionesses and seven more cubs.

From somewhere deep down in his chest, Major Temple-Boreham made a strange sound with a coaxing lilt to it. Some of the cubs looked up. One crept cautiously forward, paws flopping about as he looked for the strange new 'mother' hidden somewhere near the landrover. He walked all round us at a range of three or four yards, then came closer still, every whisker alert, sniffing and peering around the wheels.

As darkness fell, the Major switched on the spotlight. The beam lit up a fallen tree trunk about twenty yards away. In ones and twos, the cubs trooped towards it. They nosed all round then, bracing themselves with front paws against it, stretched up to peer over the top. Then they began to clamber up. The bark had long since disappeared and perhaps the grip for a small cub was not too good, for there was much scrabbling for footholds and many a tumble. Now and then a lioness would leap on to the fallen tree and walk along the

smooth curves and over the snags, carefully finding her way between the groups
of cubs. Against a background of velvety blues and violet, the tawny flanks and
the creamy-white belly of the lioness stood out boldly. The spotlight picked
out the softer shades of gold and brown of the cubs and the silver-grey of the
fallen tree. So much was happening, with about a dozen cubs on the log at any
one time, jostling for key positions, slipping off and clambering on again, that
I found it difficult to decide whether to go on watching or take my eyes off the
constantly changing pattern to scribble down some sketches.

Lion cub on a fallen tree

2nd party approaching

Keshevche 24th

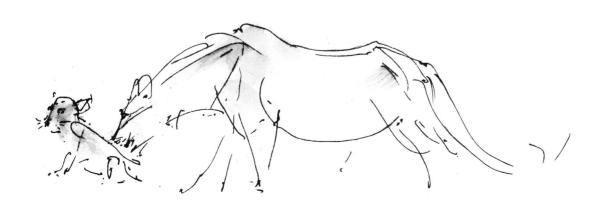

from plane at 13,000 ft   *Mt Kenya*

Samburu
Game Reserve
Kenya

Safari by Air

Oliver Brooke, who accompanied us to Samburu with his wife Betty, had most generously offered us the Company's light aeroplane for the journey, so that we would have a chance of seeing Mount Kenya at close quarters on the way. There is a physical satisfaction about flying in a light aircraft quite absent in the smooth efficiency of long-distance jets. You get a much stronger sense of buoyancy, of the bumps in the air currents and the lift of the wing as the plane banks and turns.

A front seat in the plane gave me a wonderful all-round view and the fun of watching Roy Marsh at the controls. After the thrill of the charge down the runway and the smooth lift as we were airborne, Roy gave me a running commentary on the scene below: leaving behind the blue haze of jacaranda trees around Nairobi, we flew over trim sisal fields, though some looked ragged and patchy as if people had lost heart due to competition from the man-made fibre industry; then came the Kikuyu country, small farms on hillsides, coffee plantations, banana trees, corn, the red earth dotted with thatched and corrugated

roofs. Roy dropped altitude a little, dipped the wing and I looked directly down on to a throng of brightly dressed Africans clustered around lorries and sheds where the coffee is stored and marketed, the whole scene below us like some exotic textile design.

Flying at just below cloud base the Aberdare mountains were clearly visible but the great mass of Mount Kenya was hidden by cloud cover. We followed the contours of the mountain, gaining height gradually. Farms and villages were left behind and I found myself peering down on to a dramatic landscape of giant trees, deep ravines, sheer cliffs and spectacular waterfalls. The trees appeared filmed with silvery-grey, presumably the festoons of moss and lichen. Still higher, we disappeared into cloud and when we had climbed through it, the pattern had changed to bamboo forest, and higher still to moorland and scrub.

Although we had been promised a glimpse of the summit of Mount Kenya, the cloud cover seemed impenetrable. But Roy continued to circle to the north of the mountain. Suddenly we saw the black and white of rock escarpment and snow, though the twin summits were still hidden. The plane juddered to such an extent that sketching seemed almost impossible. However, in the few moments before we banked steeply away from the mountain face, I managed to put down a few key lines which I was able to add to later.

We turned towards Samburu and were treated to one of the wonderful cloudscapes of Africa. Lit by the sun, show-white bumps of cumulus were spread across the sky, row upon row as far as the eye could see. Suddenly I was aware of a dark shape immediately ahead. The plane lifted and banked away steeply, as a bird with a huge wingspan stalled and dropped away below us. It looked like a vulture, but it all happened too quickly to be certain.

Dropping down towards Samburu, we saw floodwater straddling the middle of the airstrip. Roy said we would touch down just beyond it. And we did.

Spurwing plover

On the Equator

Africa is a land of dramatic contrasts. Sometimes a particular place will have an aura which it is very difficult to analyse: it may be either sinister and threatening, or stimulating and inviting, but always there is a feeling that there are undertones and overtones which would become clear only after long familiarity.

Our immediate reaction to Samburu, from the moment we climbed out of the plane, was a happy one: it felt light and joyous. Seeking the reasons for this is more difficult than simply recording our reactions. I can only say that as we came to know it a little better these first impressions were strengthened. The sandy earth had a gay look about it and even the greens seemed brighter than anywhere else. The skyline was ringed by the contours of hill against hill, mountain against mountain. For most of the day the summit of Mt. Kenya was hidden by a mass of dark clouds, but in the very early morning it could be seen far away to the south. The short rains were beginning; often we saw a double rainbow, arched against blue-black clouds, in vivid contrast to the bright greens of the umbrella thorns, the sunlit grass and the dry, golden bed of the Sand river.

The lodge at Samburu overlooks the swirling brown waters of the Uaso Nyiro river, at a point where tall trees line the banks. These provide shade and are also the habitat of a variety of colourful birds. Red-billed hornbills, with comical beaks and clown-like attitudes, hopped about under the trees, sending the dust flying in their search for fat grubs. One or other of a pair of African

Ground squirrels

hoopoes often joined briefly in the search and then flew back across the river to join its mate in the fork of a large tree. A pair of grey-headed kingfishers had a nest close by and they fished from a dead branch which leant out over the river. A small group of spurwing plover sunned themselves on the bank near the river by day but at dusk and in the early morning they were usually busy searching for grubs and insects around the lodge buildings.

We often watched a hammerkop (the hammer-headed stork) and a black-headed heron fishing on the opposite bank. A round shape lying over a log by the edge of the water proved to be a large turtle. We managed to capture a young leopard tortoise which scrabbled a vigorous protest during its compulsory spell as a model before being returned to its freedom at the edge of the river. A fine monitor lizard, about six feet long and beautifully decorated with white rosettes at intervals along its back, was so bold that it gave me time for a few studies before it slid away into the water. Agama lizards seemed to be every-where; the male with an orange head which deepens to brick-red according to the zest of its love life, the female less showy but with an intricate patterning along its back.

One or two of the many ground squirrels had learnt to do a brisk business with the guests after meals in the restaurant. They came right into the open veranda of the dining-room and took any food thrown to them. I got used to drinking coffee with my sketchbook open on my knee, ready to jot down some reminders of their quick movements and inquisitive attitudes. Vervet monkeys looked down from the trees nearby, also watching for a chance either to make friends—or make a raid; if they came too close, however, they were sent scampering away by the waiters.

head up - tail up.
agama lizard.

African Hoopoe

At nightfall, the sound of cicadas was intense. As we passed one particular shrub on our evening walk to the restaurant, the din was so painful that I found myself putting my hands over my ears. Fortunately, by the time we were ready to go to bed the chorus had died down. Now and then there would be mysterious rustlings from the grass roof but our mosquito nets seemed to offer a protective veil, and we were lulled to sleep by the comforting ripple of the river.

One night we woke to a great splashing from the river, as if a herd of beasts were right outside our room. When we stole out on to the veranda, all we saw was the massive black silhouette of a solitary buffalo wading strongly upstream, the moonlight sparkling on the surge of water from its limbs.

Whenever we looked out during the night, a group of waterbuck would be grazing quietly at the rear of the lodge and often there was a pair of dik-dik, the tiny antelopes, nearby. But they disappeared into the bush when the lodge awoke soon after dawn. We heard lions on several nights but saw little sign of them. Death seemed remote at Samburu.

Red-billed Hornbill.

Monitor lizard

browsing position
on hind legs

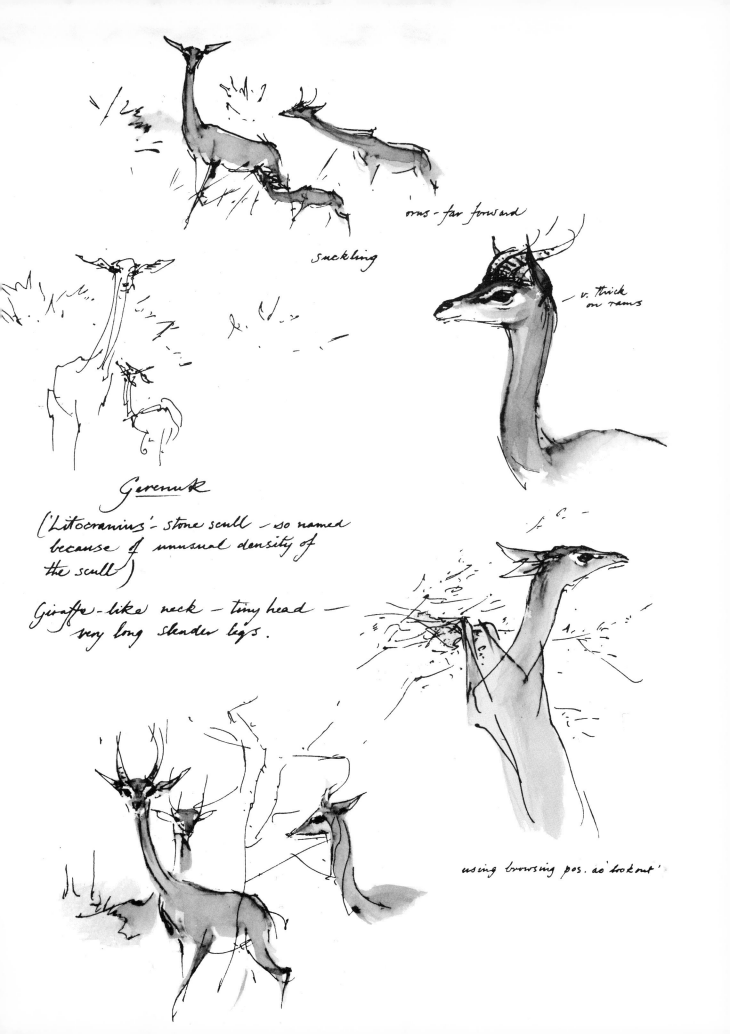

'orns - far forward

suckling

— v. thick
on rams

Gerenuk

('Litocranius' - stone scull - so named
because of unusual density of
the scull)

Giraffe-like neck - tiny head —
very long slender legs.

using browsing pos. as 'lookout'

Beisa oryx —

oxpeckers + giraffe

grevy's + waterbuck

Grevy's zebra

Dwarf Mongoose Colony
in Termite hill

Backs chocolate brown - short tails

chameleon
(about 8" long.)

Vulturine guinea fowl.

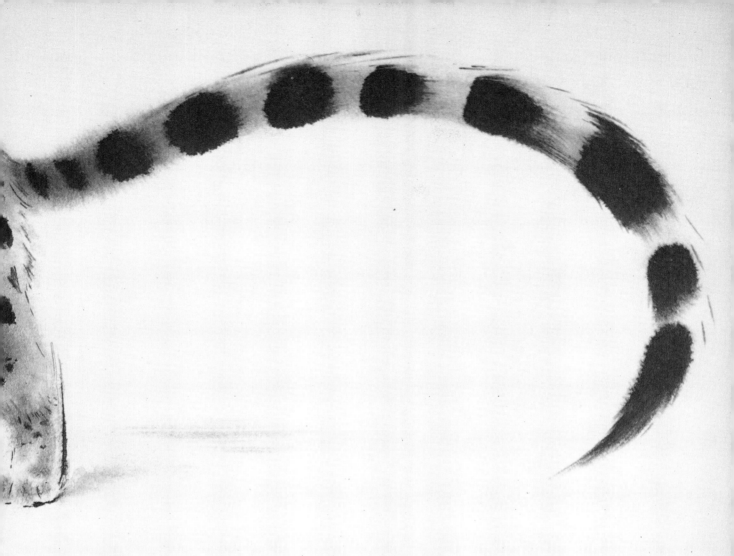

Genets

Chris Howden, manager of the Samburu Lodge, and his wife Taddy, showed a lively interest in my work. Birds were one of his specialities, and he often sat with my wife and I near the bird-table, identifying the different species for us. Taddy was more interested in animals and this made possible an opportunity for sketching wildlife which I shall always treasure.

One evening, soon after nightfall, I knocked on the Howden's door as they had asked me to do. Taddy led me to her study, a tiny room lined with books from floor to ceiling. She made me sit in her chair at the small table, so that I was facing the open window with my sketchbook beautifully lit by her Tiffany's lamp. The coloured glass shade cast a rich shadow over the bookshelves, concentrating my vision on the few objects on the table: a silver cigarette case, a dozen sharpened pencils in a vase, the *Notebooks of Dylan Thomas* at my elbow. Taddy had put a plate on the window sill, on which were a left-over meat sandwich and some apple pie. 'The genets will come when I put on a record,' explained Taddy. The strains of a Bach suite played on John Williams' guitar flowed from the sitting-room and out through the window into the darkness.

Twenty minutes went by. I kept my eyes moving over the books to prevent them from becoming too rigidly fixed on the white rectangle of the window. In the moonlit space outside, I caught sight of a shadowy golden shape. A striped hyena, the first I had ever seen, was looking round to see what it could scavenge. I knew that whilst the hyena was there, the genets would not come for their supper. Luckily it soon moved off. Ten minutes went by. Suddenly, there was a genet on the window sill, soon joined by a younger one. The two genets went for the plate of food, and immediately I was absorbed in sketching.

Almost entirely nocturnal the genet cats are interesting from the zoological angle because they are not regarded as 'true cats' but as viverrids, like the civet. In my own private classification, I regard it as half wild cat, half mongoose; and in my artist's language, a study in lithe forms and long flowing curves of spine and tail which move in interrelated shapes like music.

But I am still left wondering why a carniverous genet should prefer apple pie to meat sandwich.

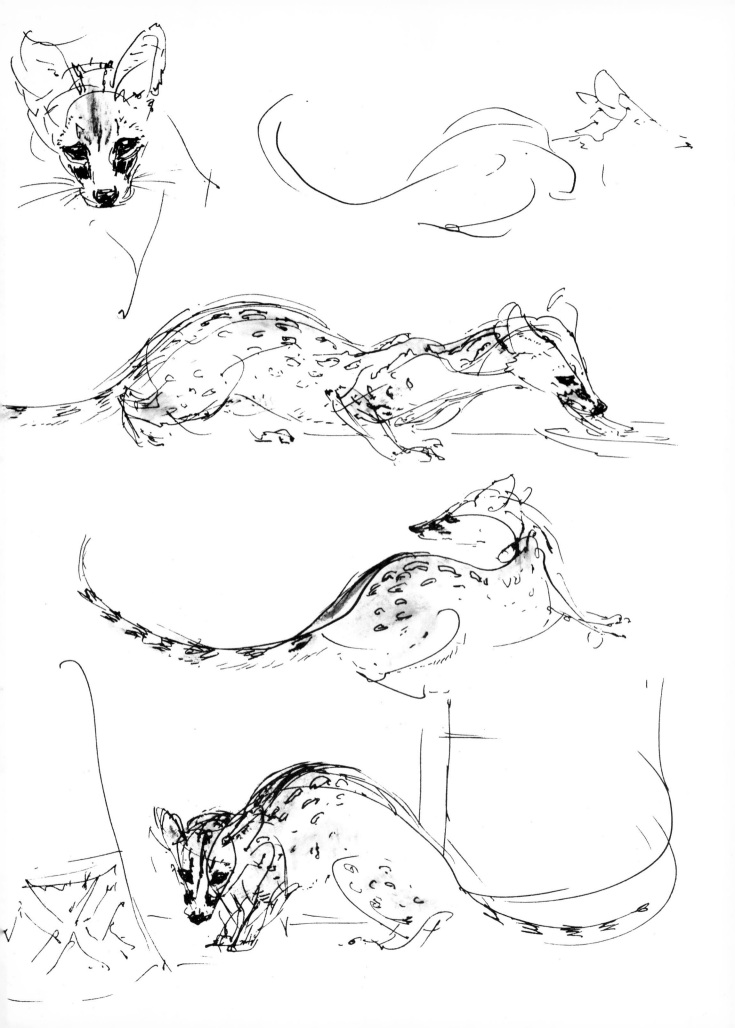

The return flights from Samburu to Nairobi and then from Nairobi to London inevitably put many thousands of miles between me and the African bush, and I was left sorting the drawings which had piled up day by day while on safari.

I found I had a particular affection for one drawing. As a rule we had no difficulty in getting quite close to lions in the car, but there was one exception. One morning, at the Masai Mara, we saw a lioness some distance away beyond a gully and crossed over to investigate. We were very much hampered by evergreen shrubs which provided dense cover. At last we caught sight of her, but at once she slipped away and Martin had to manoeuvre the car over impossible terrain to find her again. For some reason this lioness evaded our every approach and a long game of hide-and-seek followed in which the lioness had all the advantages.

Once only, she stood for a moment or two eyeing us warily from the cover of a bush before disappearing. After an hour's pursuit and with only one sketch of part of her head to show for it, we wearied of her elusiveness and left her in peace.

When we regained our starting point I looked back. Two rounded ears and a golden head gleamed among the dark greens of surrounding shrubs and bushes and a pair of narrowed eyes were watching every move we made.

Looking at the drawing now, it seems to me that the mysterious essence of the wildlife of Africa remains just as elusive as this lioness, but the enjoyment of the attempt to track it down and the studies which must of necessity remain incomplete—these were ample reward.

Lake Manyara 15ᵗʰ Oct.